A LIVING LOSS: Surviving Separation From a Loved One

A LIVING LOSS: Surviving Separation From a Loved One

Barbara Rombough, M.Ed.

Order this book online at www.trafford.com
or email orders@trafford.com

Most Trafford titles are also available at major online book retailers.

Author Credits: www.innerguidedhealing.com

Printed in the United States of America.

ISBN: 978-1-4269-4113-9 (sc)
ISBN: 978-1-4269-5735-2 (e)

Library of Congress Control Number: 2011902014

Trafford rev. 05/05/2011

www.trafford.com

North America & International
toll-free: 1 888 232 4444 (USA & Canada)
phone: 250 383 6864 • fax: 812 355 4082

TO MY MOTHER...

I feel blessed to share an interesting and loving relationship with my mother. At age eighty-nine she remains an inspiration to family and friends as she continues her independent and deeply meaningful life.

ACKNOWLEDGEMENTS

I particularly want to thank Susan J. Lunney, artist, teacher and editor, who not only expertly edited this book with a keen sense of the readers' needs; she also made it a joyful experience. As well, Susan produced a wonderful piece of cover art, which so skilfully introduces, visually, the content of my book. I thank my special circle of friends who have supported my journey in so many ways. Thanks to my husband, son and daughter in law for loving and understanding me. To my daughter's valuable input, technical skills and love which enriched my 'writing life'.

Epigraph

"I am driven forward into an unknown land
The pass grows steeper
The air colder and sharper
A wind from my unknown destination stirs
  The strings of expectation.

Still the question: Shall I ever get there?"

These are the last words of a college president's farewell address. He had been forced to relinquish his cherished position. With these final words he collapsed and died.

....Dr. Robert Ramsey's book, Living Losses: A Dramatic New Breakthrough in Grief.

Forward By Shauna Foote, M.Ed.

I remember it well – in fact, I doubt I will ever forget it. The year was 2000 and I was on top of the world. I was a young woman about to enter graduate school and at the time, I felt I had the world by the tail. I was also blessed to have two very close friends, one I had met during my undergraduate degree, four years earlier, and one I had been best friends with for twenty years. The three of us were inseparable, and those women were like family to me. I was close with their families and they were close with mine. We spent every weekend together and travelled often. One of these women even had her daughter on my birthday! Then, one day, for reasons even 10 years later I do not understand, the two of them went away on a trip without telling me and when they returned they ended their friendship with me. I was heartbroken. The break was sudden and unexpected, and I was left feeling like the rug had been pulled out from under me. Not only did I lose my two best friends, I also lost the connections with their families – people I had known my whole life. Indeed, my own family felt the loss as they too had known these women for many years and considered them family. I was in the middle of a confusing ripple effect. The whole event was painful and unfortunate, and what I did not understand at the time was that I was part of an enforced separation, and that I was grieving. I did not have the tools to properly deal with this event – instead I was filled with shame and bewilderment. I questioned my self-worth and had to work hard to forge new friendships when I believed I wasn't worthy of having them. It was not until years later, in therapy, I understood how this living loss had affected me. It is because of this event, and other similar events when I have helped clients, during the past ten years, that I became interested in living loss.

Loss and grief are natural elements of life. As human beings, we experience a variety of our own losses throughout our lifetimes, and we all experience grief in some form or another. As clinicians, we are often faced with the grieving of others. In fact, many clients who come to us are dealing with grief and loss, even if they do not initially understand that. Grief and loss can be linked to a host of difficulties, such as physical ailments, sleep disturbances, trust issues, relationship problems, just to name a few. This is why it is vital for counsellors to develop a tool kit that allows us to identify grief and help guide our clients towards resolution. We need to be able to walk our clients down the path towards healing, which begins with identifying the possible loss or grief they are dealing with. We have to be able to think outside of the box – grief does not only involve the death of a loved one. It can be the result of a loss of a relationship, the loss of employment, the loss of one's financial stability. There are so many reasons that will cause a client to grieve and we as counsellors must be able to identify and understand them. This is why a book like Barbara Rombough's A LIVING LOSS: Surviving Separation From a Loved One is such an essential tool.

A LIVING LOSS: Surviving Separation From a Loved One identifies a very common but not often discussed type of loss – enforced separation. Ms. Rombough clearly explains what this type of loss involves, which is essential information for clinicians and clients alike. This book is written much like a work-book, designed for anyone who has experienced an enforced separation, which makes it an excellent tool for counsellors. Clients can use the book to work through unresolved or newly discovered grief in a developmentally sequential manner. Each chapter builds upon the one before, and allows clients to work at a pace with which they are comfortable. Personally, one of my favourite aspects of this book is the gentle manner in which it approaches the subject. Clients will feel safe and respected while working through and processing their grief. The anecdotal story that is included in A LIVING LOSS also allows the client to relate to someone else who has "been there", which for some people will be very helpful.

A LIVING LOSS: Surviving Separation From a Loved One can also be a useful tool in building the client-counsellor relationship. You can work through the book together, and the questions in the book can be used to guide your sessions together. While exploring these questions, trust-building can occur and an understanding of this often unspoken loss can develop.

Whether you are a counsellor looking for a useful tool to add to your repertoire, or a person dealing with an enforced separation, you will find A LIVING LOSS: Surviving Separation From a Loved One a very useful book to have. I would encourage you to read through this book more than once so that you can really drink in its essence and understand the source of your grief. Do the work – answer the questions and do the exercises contained in this book with honesty and fervour. You will be glad that you did. You will learn more about yourself and begin the journey towards healing that you deserve.

Contents

Introduction

Physical loss through death is painful and distressing. This grief is most often resolved. ***The loss of a living relationship is soul wounding.*** Resolution is difficult and sorrow often remains deep. Serious mental and physical symptoms need to be addressed. Mindful based and cognitive strategies as well as relaxation techniques can help you heal and avoid serious illnesses. Unresolved grief can lead to a fatal physical outcome.

There is no right or wrong way to grieve. There are no parameters set around the time to mourn. It is a unique and personal experience. Traditionally, we speak of a loss when a person close to us dies. This is a physical loss. We will never see that person in a living dimension again. It is a time of bereavement. We are surrounded by friends, family, co-workers and community. People offer support both formally and informally when we experience the physical loss of a loved one.

Losses are experienced in other ways, such as losing a job, a friend, or our health. There are losses with moving, becoming chronically ill, we become incapacitated or incarcerated. Mentally, emotionally, physically and spiritually we incur losses. There are many ***living losses.***

A living loss is different. This book focuses on the exploration of a living loss in a situation where a person becomes estranged (the **enforced**) from a family member (the **enforcer**). Simply, we are discussing the experience of a living person, who loses an important relationship with someone. That is, someone in the family has firmly stated that he/she no longer wants contact (***the* enforcer)** with a close family member ***(the enforced)*** – they refuse to see that person. This is devastating and deeply wounding. It is a grief that is very difficult to resolve because that person is living but is not accessible. The dynamics around this situation are complex. ***Outside the family, the enforcer could be a friend, a co-worker or a partner.***

When comparing the similarities and differences between a living loss and a physical loss, it is evident that the scale is extremely unbalanced. ***There is an abundance of support for those grieving the physical death of a person, very little for those experiencing a living loss.*** It often seems that the only similarity is the experience of a painful loss.

As noted, there are many living losses. This book is focused on the enforced loss of a family member. Strategies presented help resolve the grief incurred with any living loss - grieving that is prolonged by the lack of a support system, including that of the family.

With enforced estrangement from a family member, it is important to note that, as well as the lack of support and perceived physical distancing from the extended family there is also apparent denial as to the depth of the existing estrangement and the end of an important relationship with someone. The family is often not there emotionally for the enforced person who has feelings of betrayal, having lost trust in them. Emotional connection is extremely important in any relationship. Estrangement is not the choice of the enforced person. It has been imposed by the enforcer. It is a very painful experience for which closure is extremely difficult. The person mourned for is still living. There is very little or no support for the bereaved person.

Frequently, family members choose not to discuss the situation with the enforced person. They wish to remain connected with the enforcer. One socialized myth implies that through ***thick and thin*** the family needs to stay together. Often this perception leads to feelings of guilt and results in the estranged person choosing not to share the experience with others. The enforced feels vulnerable when approaching family members only to be met with a negative response.

Feelings of betrayal and guilt are extremely deep. To suddenly be an outsider is a painful living ***loss.***

Chapter I

Going with the Flow: Living Losses

"Stand like mountain. Flow like water".
Brian Luke Seaward

Recently the verb ***iced*** has been used in the context of becoming disconnected from someone through being cast out of a relationship. That is, being ***iced*** by a friend, partner or family member. For those who have experienced this pain, it is not an exaggeration to say that the body, mind and spirit feel frozen while one flounders alone through the journey of grief and enforced estrangement.

As a therapist, I began thinking about clients who have lived through the experience of a ***living loss.*** I realized how very infrequently they disclosed or discussed the pain that occurred after being enforced from someone's life. In an *AHA moment,* I realized that they were probably not talking about the loss with anyone.

Prior to that moment, in my practice, I had presented an eclectic mix of strategies that often focused on cognitive/reality therapy. I introduced working questions such as, "What do I want?", "What am I doing to get what I want?", "Is it working?", "If not, what can I do differently?", "What are my needs and strengths?", "What thinking do I need to change?" and "What is my plan?"

These strategies are a successful approach for therapy. Yet, for some clients, I felt I was missing the mark. There was a density of loss and pain that could not be touched. I sensed that I needed to develop a structured approach that included an assessment for the presence of a living loss.

As I continued to explore my thinking, I visualized myself with my clients at our first session. I noted that initially I asked which distress symptoms (sleeplessness, lack of concentration, anger, and so on) he/she was presently experiencing. I did not include and define the question: ***Are you grieving the loss of someone, or something through an enforced estrangement?*** Or, ***are you estranged from a family member?*** I continued to explore the phenomenon and decided I would ask similar questions, in the future, regardless of what problems were being discussed.

It is my belief that depression, anxiety, stress, burnout, and other indicators including those of physical illness, may be revealed because of unresolved living losses. For those who have experienced such a devastating loss – first, and most importantly, it is essential to listen to their story. People need to know that their feelings, were and still are, valid. There are deep emotions most often difficult to resolve.

In time, those who are resolving a living loss need to begin observing themselves within the context of relationships, and to resist feeling like a ***victim*** while exploring the lost relationship. Important information and coping strategies are found later in this book. Research indicates that there is a high risk for terminal/chronic disease and acute illnesses, like cancer, and heart disease for those living with unresolved grief. This knowledge is a serious motivation for seeking resolution.

Grief is a journey of the self. Grieving occurs within different time parameters, bringing diverse and undesired mental and physical consequences to each person. Sophie's experience, as a fictional character, allows me to present my observations. I am able to share with you the healing process necessary in order to resolve the grief of enforced estrangement. Her story is anecdotal (information in the form of a narrative). It gives a background from which we begin to understand how the experience of an enforced relationship can happen to us. When we become aware of the complexities and depth in the structure of any family, we can gain more understanding, move out of the shock stage and begin healing.

Sophie's experience of illness, in relation to grief, became very real. At age 45, more than two years after the enforced estrangement from her brother, she became ill and required surgery. Previously she had never had an illness. Her physician indicated that considering her symptoms, the odds of cancer were extremely high. She was very ill during the eight weeks before her surgery.

She spent her days practicing visualization, meditation, praying and doing relaxation techniques such as deep breathing and deep muscle relaxation. These helped to control her fears and the pain. Frequent thoughts of the enforced estrangement from her brother, as well as the pain of this loss interrupted her meditation.

The emotional pain was devastating as she replayed the story over and over in her mind, on a daily basis. She relived a small part of her childhood in an unhappy home where she and her brother were close. She had protected him from their father's anger, and continued to do so over the years. She helped him when he was in trouble, and needed a shoulder to cry on. Again, she questioned how he could have shunned her in such a cold way, through an e-mail.

As Sophie continued her journey of sad recollections, she traveled the path of her early adulthood. She had always felt unloved and on the outside of things, especially within the family. She remembered the exact time when she decided to work on herself. She went to self-development courses, and learned yoga which she continued to practice. As she became a more assured person, she couldn't understand why her relationship with her family members became more and more difficult. Sometimes she felt that the pain and confusion were too much to bear. Sophie was also grieving for her very good friend who had previously died. Her loss remained unresolved, as she recovered from surgery.

At her follow up appointment, six weeks after surgery, her surgeon told her that she was a very lucky woman. Although surgery had revealed a large ovarian tumour, the biopsy results indicated there was no cancer. While recuperating, she decided to work on resolving her grief from the loss of her friend. She began reading Dr. Robert Ramsay's book, Living with Loss (see bibliography) and learned about living ***losses***. She realized that first she had to resolve the loss of her relationship with her brother, the enforcer who had terminated their connection. Sophie had had no contact with him for three years. Still in shock, she couldn't believe that her brother had ended their relationship.

She decided to do what was necessary to resolve the loss of her important relationship. Psychologically, she still experienced deep emotional pain and many sad and painful triggers, when looking at family pictures, having conversations about, and remembering situations with, the enforcer. She realized that she was still very much feeling ***the victim***.

As the ***enforced person*** Sophie focused on Ramsey's book. She quickly became aware of the trauma of a living loss. The beginning of chapter one, Grief: Life's Unavoidable Companion distressed her when the author described the experience of a college president who was giving his farewell speech. He had been coerced into relinquishing his cherished position through the petty politics of the college administration.

In the preface of Ramsay's book, Sophie had read a quote of the professor's last few words and actions. "Hesitantly, stepping back from the podium, he sank to his knees, whimpering his last breath before the horrified eyes of the stricken audience and the stunned Board of Governors who had forced his ouster." **He died immediately.**

Did the unresolved pain of losing his presidency (a living loss) cause his death? As Dr. Ramsey says, "We will never know". However, he does say that research is now connecting body and mind - in this case grief, to physical illness. Ramsey states " ......there is a connection between grief and death as undeniable as life itself".

After reading Robert Ramsay's book, Sophie ***knew*** that she had to begin healing. Using her own experience, and what she had learned from Dr.

Ramsay, she began a healing path when she started reading this book, ***A LIVING LOSS: Surviving Separation From a Loved One.***

Sophie came to accept that a relationship consists of two people, neither one devoid of responsibility for the estrangement. With this recognition of her own feelings, Sophie began to open herself up to strategies and knowledge that hastened her journey through grief resolution to healing. Initially, it was very difficult for her to be a neutral observer. She was experiencing all the emotions of grief.

The experience of a living loss is very deep and extremely painful. There is no closure. The enforcer who instigated the estrangement is still living and yet unattainable. It is important to examine the way we behave socially when it comes to a ***physical loss,*** compared to a ***living loss.*** At a young age, we learn about giving and receiving support for a physical loss, but do not learn about a living loss.

Chapter II

Sorrow Unmasked: Helping Those Who Grieve

"Your joy is your sorrow unmasked.
The deeper that sorrow carves into your being,
the more joy it can contain".
Kahlil Gibran

In the therapeutic world of grieving, it is suggested that, ***how*** we grieve the physical death of a loved one is influenced by the ideas we adopt as we journey through life. These are often expressed through the language we use to comfort grieving persons.

Phrases such as, "Time heals all wounds", "God never gives us more than we can bear" and "Be strong for others", are often used to console our friends and family as they struggle through the grieving process.

It is ***suggested*** that these messages teach us ***not*** to feel badly, to replace the loss in some way, keeping busy helps, and grieving alone is acceptable in our society. We are uncomfortable with loss as a society. As children, we are told to leave others alone when they are sad, or we may have been sent to our room to cry. Some of us have even heard; "If you are going to cry – go to your room", "Big boys/girls don't cry", "Be strong for __________".

We often hear words that prevent us from expressing our sad feelings. "Get hold of yourself. You can't fall apart", are often part of the repertoire. We may even be told harshly, "I'll give you something to cry about". We remember these messages as we grow older. This is the pattern we use to ***help*** others.

The way we deal with death is the way we deal with life. We use platitudes because we seem to be uncomfortable with the sad feelings of others as well as our own. Habitually, we don't know what to say or do when someone is grieving. As a result, we resort to the comfortable clichés. These words may appear to be inept, nevertheless, when someone dies they do provide us with a means to offer our sympathies and condolences to the survivors. ***There are very few such words for those grieving a living loss.***

With a ***physical loss,*** support is offered through words as well as the indication that we are available for that person if, and when, they wish to talk. We listen and empathize with them when they have doubts. We are there for those who are grieving, as they tell the details of their story. This life review is a very important component of the grief process.

The ritual that surrounds the death of a loved one serves to bring us a sense of comfort and shared grief, during these very difficult losses. We may share in the viewing of the body during visiting hours, attend the funeral, the reception and the procession to the cemetery. Our attendance provides a ritual of closure of these very last ***rites of passage*** for the deceased person.

When everyone has left and the rituals have ended, friends remain connected and offer support. Our faith and therapy become other options for the grieving person. At this time, ***core-distress symptoms such as sleeplessness, poor appetite, lack of concentration, anger, and extreme sadness*** may continue to plague the bereaved individual. They may look for support from professionals.

There is a good possibility that support will continue whether or not the grieving person seeks professional help or is referred by a professional. One of the most painful life experiences is the physical loss of a loved one. The experience is different for each person. Friends and family gather together, regardless of the relationship that had existed with the deceased, and the grieving person.

A network of support provides the bereaved person with the opportunity to do a ***life review.*** The opportunity to tell others about life experiences with the deceased person is a critical grief resolution. The stories are told many times to different people. The continuing support offered is necessary to allow a full closure of the relationship that has ended through death.

Chapter III

An Inner Journey: Losses

"Grieving is physical as well as spiritual. It is an inner journey, but its restlessness demands movement".
Barbara Lazear Ascher

As previously noted, there are many losses that do not include physical death, such as, ***the loss of a job, a marriage, a family relationship, a loss of health, or financial security.*** All indicate bereavement. These are crises that need to be processed and resolved. Usually the more grief work we can complete, the shorter will be the grieving period. These losses can be viewed as 'living losses' or psychic losses. There is much less support provided than that for a physical loss.

A lost relationship is a living loss. There has been a total estrangement between two family members. Let us consider a situation where a dominant family member (enforcer) has forcibly separated him/herself from a close relative with absolutely no contact. This person has discerned that the other person is not worth a relationship. Often this severing of ties is completed through a family messenger, a letter, or an email, not in person. Other extended family members will often follow an unwritten directive by the enforcer. In this situation there is usually very little or no support for the enforced, who has lost an important relationship.

Relationships are a basic component of our lives. They are connections that involve every part of our existence. Through relationships we gain our sense of who we are, and how we fit into the world around us. They work to help us know and understand what is authentic and what is a priority in our life.

We become very anxious and insecure when relationships end. These feelings are magnified when the break has been enforced upon us. We experience a crisis of connectedness. When we lose the sense of who we are, we feel anxiety and sometimes lose our sense of reality. We experience a tremendous amount of shock, stress, and grief during the loss of this relationship.

Frequently, the enforced relationship loss is an area where the necessary grief work is ***not done***. This loss may be a total shock. It may happen in a relationship where the person has felt out of place and slighted by the enforcer. The reasons for enforced estrangements are not always clear. There may be a co-dependency within the immediate and extended family members who are frequently entangled in each others lives. When we explore this situation, we note a lack of direct communication where family members are expected to think the same way.

This type of family relationship almost ensures that, eventually someone will be ***ostracized*** from the group. The enforcer may have a history of removing others from the midst of his/her space. It is probably not the first time. When this happens, family members are known to form an alliance in order to retain their own place in the family unit.

This loyalty means that the family will often gather collectively when the enforcer perceives that a certain person has become intolerable and needs to be banned. Most likely there will be little or no emotional support provided to the person who has suffered an ***enforced relationship.***

There may be small pockets of hidden alliances for the excluded person. This further confuses the already fragile and estranged person. ***Open*** support for the enforced is not likely. As indicated earlier, funeral rituals and the support, and all that comes with them are very important factors in the processing of grief, when one experiences the physical loss of a relationship. This support is essential. As noted, a most important process in grieving is the ***life review*** which is the story of the relationship repeated many times, to many people.

It is the ***lack*** of three main factors that complicate and extend the grieving process when a person experiences a relationship living loss:

1) The lack of any ritual display

2) The lack of open communication and support from family members

3) The prevention of a life review for the person grieving.

To this list, we can add the feelings of guilt and responsibility that the enforced person feels for breaking the myth that the family must remain together regardless of circumstances. ***This most often prevents the person from reaching out to family, friends, or professionals. It blocks the healing process.***

While it is understandable that there are no rituals for this loss, it is difficult to understand the scarcity of emotional support from family members that is devastating to the bereaved person. This blocks the grieving process, disallowing the hurt person from talking about the personal loss, the relationships involved and the feelings experienced. It is overwhelming and destructive. Feeling a lack of support, the grieving person usually moves into a pathological bereavement, experiencing a helplessness to discuss their grief with anyone.

Chapter IV

Finding Your Centre: Unresolved Grief

"Be still and discover your centre of peace."
Lao Tzu

Pathological bereavement is an almost unavoidable consequence when a person is denied these rituals for grieving. In particular, the psychological outlet of talking about the loss is necessary for the resolution of grief. The person who is experiencing a ***living or psychic loss*** often cannot resolve this grief through a life review with support of others. There is usually a high risk of physical illness in their future.

As stated earlier, the more actively grief work is done, the shorter will be the grieving period. Psychic loss leads to pathological bereavement since the tools necessary for this process are denied the grieving person.

In his book, Living with Loss, Ronald W. Ramsay states that there is abundant research indicating the correlation between unresolved grief and illness. One study indicates that 72% of adult cancer patients, as early as six months to a span of 9 years prior to the illness, had experienced a significant psychic, or living loss.

Dr. David Servan-Schreiber, MD, PhD, presents a more recent picture of the "mind/body link". He states that there is indisputable evidence emerging in this area of research. In his book, Anticancer: A New Way of Life, he states that when the Lancet (a prestigious medical journal) published Dr. Irvin Yalom's research, the suggestion of definitive proof "between mental state and the development of disease", transitioned from a "new age" concept to being a highly respected scientific hypothesis.

In 2006, Dr. Servan-Schreiber states that a longitudinal study undertaken in Finland, indicates the particular importance of using the research variable "the feeling of helplessness", not just for cardiac disease but for all cases of mortality and notably cancer. This was a study in which participants were initially healthy.

A wide scale meta-analyses of 165 studies published in 2008 by psychologists at the University College London, confirmed the Finland research results. They defined the term "psychosocial stress" which included the death of close family members and divorce. Most notably, feelings of helplessness were among the reactions to these events. For a deeper understanding of the phenomenon, one ought to consider reading Dr. Schreiber's book.

In simple terms, psychological stress leads to the release of cortisol, a stress hormone, which disturbs the balance of immune cells and inhibits the normal response to the presence of abnormal cells. In turn, immune cells release signals which affect the brain and influence behavior. As a result, when a person gives up, the immune system dramatically reduces its protective function in the body. In the last twenty years, a new scientific link between psychological factors and the activity of the immune system has emerged. The initial study in Finland began with the question "What is the feeling of helplessness?"

What could be a more helpless feeling than being in an enforced separation from a loved-one? Those who have experienced this event seem caught in a hopeless and helpless situation. When an enforced breakup takes place, the offended person is often totally preoccupied by memories of the person who so quickly removed him/her from the family. The estranged person feels a negative attitude from family members who have reacted in what appears to be support of the ***enforcer*** and not the ***enforced*** or grieving person.

Often the message perceived is that he or she is neurotic and at the root of the problem. A painful journey of self doubt and second guessing begins. The affected person has likely been feeling a loss for some time. The need to be loved is strong. With no communication or understanding, it is not likely that any needs will be filled.

Deep and honest communication is unlikely between the enforced person and the family, when a social myth indicates that families must stick together. The wounded person may deny the situation and accept the blame for an uncomfortable relationship. The lesson learned very early, in co-dependent families, is that if he/she wants to belong, it is necessary to stay within the beliefs and opinions of the family. Choosing to be in conflict with the enforcer may lead to exclusion.

Enforced persons who have chosen to remain silent may have a tendency to gradually disengage from a painful and uncomfortable relationship. They might attempt to see the enforcer less frequently. Setting these boundaries for the relationship often magnifies the family perception that the enforced person is ***difficult.***

Change is frightening. When a vulnerable person begins to grow and change in a co-dependent family, his/her progress is not tolerated well. Initially this person may be excluded from information and events concerning the family. The next step is likely to be enforced estrangement for the person who is perceived as troublesome. This may be a sibling, or an extended family member.

Often after removing the offending person mentally and emotionally, physical exclusion, by refusal to see the enforced, results. When verbal expression of true feelings is attempted by the enforced, the break in the relationship may be quickly made by the enforcer through a letter or an e-mail. In this environment, the concept that everyone is allowed an opinion is not supported. The idea that we may dislike someone's behaviour without disliking the person is an unfamiliar idea.

Sadly, the extended family offers little or no support to someone who is enforced. The entire family, although fully aware of the situation, typically offers no solace and/or refuses to comment, when the excluded person seeks support.

The support needed at this time is validation and affirmation of feelings, regardless of what they are. Those grieving a living loss are not ready to be faced with questions like: "What are the positive aspects of this relationship?" "Is it more beneficial to focus on the positive relationships around you?" ***The deepest need for the estranged person, is to hear that, he/she is a worthy, competent, lovable, and deserving person.***

Rather than providing the necessary support to the enforced through reminiscing, family members may state, "You'd better fix this situation" or "Forget about it" or "I'm not taking sides" or "It is your fault, stop talking about it". Any number of unsupportive comments or total silence may be the grieving person's experience.

The painful silence is devastating to an enforced person who is a ***wounded soul.*** The alienated person feels judged and disrespected. Prior to this time, there may have been periods of depression or more positively, a journey of self development might have begun. Perhaps the affected person has been working to grow emotionally. However, there is a deep pain experienced by the offended person. The grief is not only sustained through the break in the relationship, it is magnified by the lack of support the enforced person receives from the extended family. At this point, without resolution of grief, the person has entered a pathological grieving state.

It is necessary to understand clearly the **differences** between grieving the ***physical loss*** of a loved one and the ***living loss*** of a loved one. ***In a living loss:***

- guilt and shame most often remain and extend throughout the acute stage of grieving
- family rules and taboos can cause deep denial and self blame which often prevents resolution of the grief The bereaved person often does not reach out to family, friends or professionals
- lack of support for, and self isolation of, the grieving person from the family, prevents resolution through talking about the relationship.

These three factors often prevent the beginning of the grieving process. The ***shock*** stage of grieving a living loss lasts much longer. It continues long into the acute and resolution stage of grieving. Remaining in the shock stage of grief extends the experience of prolonged core distress symptoms. This will be discussed in a later chapter.

Chapter V

Erosion of Sorrow: The Journey of Grief

"Sorrow. Like the river, must be given vent lest it erodes its bank."
Earl A. Grollman

An ***emotional trigger*** may be positive or negative. It is a thought, or feeling, initiated by one or a number of situations. A sound, smell, sight or touch may trigger a reaction. As well, a memory, a flash-back, a photograph or a familiar gathering can stimulate certain feelings. A particular time of year, especially festive seasons and certain anniversary dates, may bring remembrance of shared occasions with others in the past.

With a living loss, ***negative emotions*** are stirred since the estrangement is extremely painful to the enforced person. Feelings experienced may be sadness, anger, betrayal, guilt, resentment or shame. As well, a general sense of physical malaise and depression may exist. The lack of support from extended family members magnifies these mood swings, increasing the susceptibility for serious physical illnesses. A living loss is more likely to set in action feelings of self-blame and shame. These emotional triggers often extend grief resolution and are much longer lasting.

The grievers of ***living losses*** do not have the opportunity to share emotions concerning the enforcer. They often do not even have the option of mentioning his/her name, or, expressing their feelings as they grieve. Through the pain of loss, they feel the need to say, "I think I saw (the enforcer) the other day", "I was sure that I heard his/her foot-step on the stairs", or "When I see a blue car, my heart skips a beat". Not sharing this prevents the processing of grief, which lies like a lump in the chest and the throat.

Memories and flashbacks continue as the bereaved person lives in a lonely void where even a name brings deep pain. A major negative trigger may occur when there is a discussion regarding the estranged person's friends, children, grandchildren or there are stories of family activities and reunions. These happy events initiate grief for the enforced and provide a constant reminder of the loss of an important relationship, as well as the perceived betrayal of other family members.

It is ***important*** to acknowledge triggers, and assess their strength as the grieving process continues. Some triggers remain even after grief is resolved. We know that certain situations were painful in the past, but are not at the present time. Knowing that we have moved on with our lives, we can make choices not to react emotionally to negative thoughts and feelings. We have learned to change our thinking through certain cognitive coping strategies, including reality therapy, introduced in a later section.

Dr. William Glasser, MD, psychiatrist, author and founder of Choice Theory/Reality Therapy often says, "We almost always have choices, and the better the choice, the more we will be in control of our lives". We have control over our thinking and acting so sometimes we have to do something different to feel better. In a living loss, we need to change our response to the grief we experience, especially when we do not have the opportunity to share our emotions with the enforcer.

It is necessary to know and recognize the stages of grief. It is essential to believe that we ***deserve*** compassion and understanding. As previously noted, it is unlikely that we can specifically identify the reasons why this ***living loss*** has occurred. Knowing more about family rules, myths, taboos and co-dependent families can offer further understanding.

A living loss is magnified because of feelings of ***grief and shame*** when:

- we are experiencing other losses such as a divorce or miscarriage
- the relationship was toxic or dependent and unstable
- there is a scarcity of family and social support
- we do not have an opportunity to complete a relationship review with friends and family
- there is no ritual support, such as a funeral service, visitation, or a burial ceremony

Co-dependency

Co-dependency may be defined in different ways. It can describe the traits developed when a person lives in a family where there is addiction. There are specific responses and behaviours that develop with non-addicted family members.

Co-dependence also describes an unhealthy pattern of living and problem-solving in a childhood of unspoken or learned family rules and family myths which may have begun generations ago. It is something into which we are socialized. From this environment, it becomes harder **for some adults t**o have free will and express conscious desires. This person's needs are often unmet. These family members frequently need to learn appropriate assertiveness and communication skills.

Co-dependent families most often do not accept other family members who have healthy boundaries or are making changes in their lives. Rules may include:

- don't discuss our problems
- keep your feelings to your self
- indirect communication is best (often done by messengers)
- be strong, right, and perfect unrealistic expectations
- don't be selfish
- don't rock the boat
- families stick together, no matter what happens.

Society tends to support these behaviours through clichés like ***blood is thicker than water.*** These ideas live through literature, films, and songs. In the 12th and 13th century, the feeling at the time was -relationships within the family are stronger than any other kind and relatives always stick together.

Aldous Huxley contradicted this thinking by saying "***but water is wider, thank the Lord than blood.***" In the book, Jonathon Livingstone Sea Gull, David Bach offers a healthy expectation of families when he states that "***the blood that links your true family, is not of blood but of respect and joy in each other's lives.***" When we have been enforced from an important family relationship, we need to resolve our loss through learning meaningful and concise coping strategies which are presented later. The bibliography lists important books to consider reading.

We need to understand the journey. We must learn about the steps of grieving, in order to begin understanding and internalizing the process. We ***need*** the benefit of support from family, friends and the rituals that are provided when a physical death occurs. A living loss needs to be explored deeply. As a grieving person, we must understand the ***connection*** between an unresolved ***living loss*** and ***serious physical illness.*** Sharing our stories, through therapy, or talking to a willing friend or an immediate family member is a necessity. Lessening the difficulty, through therapy with a professional is recommended. Pain cuts deeply through the ostracized person who cannot seem to move forward in life until the grief is resolved.

Survivors of a lost relationship may share some of the following experiences:

- Having difficulty being heard while in a painful and difficult relationship.
- Living with unresolved grief that may last for years, often developing serious health problems as a result.
- Feeling responsible for the unhealthy dynamics and alliances within the family.
- Experiencing mental exhaustion and possibly burning out from constantly focusing on why the estrangement occurred.
- Not seeking professional guidance and support.
- Not seeking help because of family rules and taboos regarding the *sacredness* of the family, resulting in feelings of guilt and shame.

The enforced person may feel exhausted from the seemingly endless struggle to feel loved and be included in the family circle. He/she may have been seeking detachment from a family member for years before the estrangement. Because the enforced was perceived as a difficult person, the enforcer may have been oblivious to the offended person's pain and need to belong.

Knowing that the enforcer may have a past history of excluding others intensifies the fear and stress. Grieving may already have begun long before the estrangement of these family members. ***A living loss*** negatively affects the body, mind and spirit of those who have lost a relationship. The door for any communication is closed. Any contact is rejected. The loss is deep.

The estranged person's need for love and belonging is further damaged when it seems that most family members align with the enforced. Perhaps untrue, the wounded soul perceives secrecy within the family. The vulnerable, grieving person becomes exhausted from exerting tremendous energy toward dealing with lost relationships. The role of victim is felt deeply and it becomes difficult to respond rationally to the estrangement.

The estranged person might try to contact the enforcer. When there is no response, the feelings of isolation and lack of support increase, as the pain pushes deeper. At this point in the relationship the ostracized person will experience further pain and begin to accept the blame and guilt for the entire situation. The enforced person may be experiencing depression, stress, burnout, or anxiety as well as other physical symptoms.

The probability of discussing the difficulties resulting from the estrangement from a loved one is unlikely. Grieving is most often done alone. Regardless of what symptoms or problems are being revealed, it is likely that grief is the core issue. The three stages of grieving a living loss will be explored further in following chapters. At this point the stages of grieving a ***living loss*** will be referred to as stages 1, 2, and 3.

Chapter VI

Trust Yourself: Stages of Grief

"Trust Yourself. You know what you want and need."
Cherry Hartman

Becoming aware of the stages for grieving a ***living loss*** and learning strategies to help deal with the painful experience is essential. The three stages are similar to those experienced through the physical death of a loved one. These stages do not occur laterally but shift back and forth:

1. **Shock**

Emotions of grief, sadness and depression are experienced with highs and lows. There are also feelings of denial and guilt. Core distress symptoms remain unresolved.

2. **Acute stage**

In this stage, crying, emotional swings, feelings of helplessness and hopelessness, anxiety, despair and anger will likely be experienced. In a ***living loss*** feelings of shock and denial often remain strong in the acute stage. These feelings have usually dissipated, at this point when grieving the ***physical loss*** of a loved one. Each person grieves uniquely depending on his or her own life experience. There is no ***norm.***

The first step to dealing with guilt feelings is becoming aware of them. Guilt is a strong emotion. These feelings are real and need to be dealt with, but the grieving person needs to know that the ***reason for the guilt is probably not real.*** This is important validation.

A complication may arise during the acute stage. Often there are feelings of total bewilderment when the enforcer sends a message through another family member. Perhaps it has been stated that there needs to be some resolution. This situation frequently has a negative outcome because the message has been delivered by someone other than the enforcer. Perceived betrayal of the extended family is felt more keenly. Anger becomes stronger and a defensive stance begins.

3. Acceptance and Movement

The time eventually arrives when the enforced person's emotional pain is dealt with and equilibrium is finally restored. The enforced realizes that even though two or more persons shared this broken relationship, no one person is responsible for its ending. It is time to move forward.

Chapter VII

Overcoming Suffering: Physical and Living Losses

"Although the world is full of suffering, it is full also of the overcoming of it".
Helen Keller

As noted previously, the similarities and differences between a living loss and a physical loss are extremely unbalanced. There is an abundance of support for those grieving the physical death of a person, almost none for those experiencing a living loss. It seems that the only similarity is the experience of a painful loss.

As you begin the journey of healing this loss, it is important to record how your body, mind and spirit are dealing with your personal ***living loss*** of a family member. It is important to record your ***core distress symptoms and evaluate how you are doing as you begin your healing journey.*** In this way you can monitor your progress as you travel along the path of grief resolution.

How are you coping with your loss? **On a scale of 1 – 10** (1 is low, 5 is average and 10 is excellent.) ___________________________. Check your first or "base-line" scores and record them on the following journal page, as follows:

Sleeplessness
Confusion
Lack of concentration
Anger
Physical symptoms
Change in appetite (eating more or less)
Sadness
Others _________________________

Journal Entry

Date:

- Sleeplessness

  ____

- Confusion

  ____

- Lack of concentration

  ____

- Anger

  ____

- Physical symptoms

  ____

- Change in appetite (eating more or less)

  ____

- Sadness

  ____

- Others

  ____

Thoughts: (Write about what you are thinking?)

Physical Loss

Unlike a living loss, there is support for a physical loss:

- body, mind and spirit

There is emotional support with:

- words of comfort
- sympathy
- condolences

There is physical support:

- a network of family members, friends, etc., who will listen as we tell our stories
- when sharing our experiences with someone, we do a life review of the relationship with a person we trust. This is an important healing strategy
- friends and family remain connected with us after the funeral. They are present in our daily lives

There are rituals:

- funeral service
- reception
- funeral procession
- burial

When a physical loss occurs, with a support network, eventually most people grieving will resolve the loss, unless there are other difficulties. Sometimes, there may be a mental illness, a toxic relationship or other unresolved grief such as a *living loss* which prevent resolution.

Living Loss

There exists little or no emotional support for a living loss:

- the enforced person often cannot discuss the loss with friends because of shameful feelings, nor with family who fear "taking sides". They may have refused to engage in conversation about the estrangement
- family myths and rules indicate that the family must ***remain together regardless of circumstances*** which brings ***self-blame and shame*** to the enforced person
- having broken the family rule, the enforced person isolates him/herself and is unable to reach out to other family members which is a major obstacle to resolution
- the estrangement is not discussed with the family therefore the enforced person feels betrayed.

There is often ***little or no physical support*** for the grieving person, in a living loss:

- the enforced is usually distanced from other family members
- family members remain connected with the enforcer.

There is ***absolutely no ritual support*** for a living loss.

In addition to little, or no emotional, physical or ritual support, the following feelings further complicate the resolution of a living loss in a family.

There are feelings of ***self blame.*** Guilt, shame, shock and disbelief remain with the bereaved person throughout the acute stage of grieving. These feelings may be present as long as there is no grief resolution. Feeling unable to reach out to family, friends, or a professional, is devastating.

Living losses are magnified by the following which complicate, extend and prevent grief resolution:

1. lack of support from friends and family
2. lack of opportunity to talk about the lost relationship
3. lack of help from a professional person

Clearly, these conditions prevent the opportunity to do the necessary grief work. Being able to talk about the painful experience is ***crucial,*** in any resolution of loss. Although the extended family may not have totally estranged themselves physically, the enforced person has feelings of betrayal and a lack of trust. ***Self imposed detachment from the family complicates resolution.***

Although, each person is unique in his/her grief, the inability to do grief work during the bereavement, prevents resolution. In the situation of a living loss, resolution seems unlikely. The enforced will experience pathological or unresolved grief with possible physical health risks, if there is no resolution within two to three years (more or less).

Chapter VIII

Facing Unresolved Grief: Grieving Stage I

"The only grief that does not end is grief that has not been fully faced".
Judy Tatelbaum

Becoming familiar with the stages of grieving a living loss will help you acknowledge your own experience. There will be helpful strategies for you to begin resolving your grief. Read with a pencil in your hand, as you continue this part of your journey.

Similar to the loss experienced through the physical death of a loved one, the initial stages experienced are shock and denial. The most prevalent emotions experienced are sadness and depression. Numerous core distress symptoms mentioned earlier, may be present.

There are many variables which affect the grieving process, such as age, gender, relationship with the lost person, physical and mental strength, and the types of support available. When a person is experiencing unresolved grief through a living loss, it is necessary to first uncover the areas of stress which are being experienced by that person. Grieving is a most stressful and anxiety-laden experience.

Whether with a therapist or a friend, the first time the painful estrangement is discussed at any length, is a huge step. The first deep feelings are likely to be expressed when we receive validation and affirmation of our emotions. Repressed feelings will begin to surface. ***It is helpful to start some strategies at this time.***

These are important strategies:

- increasing physical exercise will promote the production of endorphins which help to elevate your mood
- focusing on **yourself** and beginning an interest such as art, music or physical activity will be beneficial
- relaxing, using techniques such as deep muscle relaxation, visualization and relaxation CD's, deep breathing and meditation are very important

Relaxation technique is any activity, or process, that helps a person to relax and reduces anxiety or stress. It is possible to reduce muscle tension, and blood pressure, as well as deepening breath and slowing heart rate, when using a relaxation exercise. Anger, anxiety, headaches, insomnia and depression can be decreased. Your general well being, cardiac health, immune system and pain management may also be improved.

You may wish to explore any or all of the following options.

- Mindfulness is any repetitive action such as, quilting, hiking, chopping wood, painting, knitting or singing. It helps you to pay attention to the present moment. Deep breathing can be a meditation when you focus on your breath and distract your thoughts.
- Advanced Mindfulness courses and books help you learn how to remain in the present through meditation by using certain breathing techniques/exercises and delaying your thoughts.
- Visualization is the technique of using your imagination. You can create a peaceful scene in your mind. Visualize anything that stops you thinking negative thoughts. This can be a beautiful place, or a feeling of touching something soft. There are visualization CD's and mental exercises you may choose to use. You can do a mini-visualization by taking a minute to

visualize something positive such as your loved one, a favorite animal or a special gathering place.

- Deep Breathing comes in many patterns and combinations. Abdominal breathing is helpful when you push out the belly while breathing in, pulling in the belly when breathing out. You may wish to create breathing patterns. You can breathe in while counting to 5, hold your breath for 5, count to 5 as you release your breath. To modify this exercise you can start at 1 breath count and continue the pattern to 10 breath counts or vary the number as you wish.
- Massage by a professional or self massage is very helpful. They are simple and quickly relieve tension (see bibliography).
- Deep muscle relaxation is easy to learn and brings profound relaxation by starting with the toes, lightly squeezing and releasing the different muscle groups, until you reach your head.
- Taking a time out is a strategy we often ignore. We over-schedule ourselves without a break. Make a commitment to taking five or ten minutes periodically throughout the day. Some suggestions are, focus on your breathing, do deep muscle relaxation, stand up tall and stretch as you walk slowly at home or at work, inside or outside. The time can be expanded as you feel more comfortable.
- Relaxation music can 'slow down the heartbeat and soothe the soul'.
- Reducing Caffeine found in tea, coffee, chocolate, and soft drinks, is necessary for a calmer life and sounder sleep.
- Feel Affection by cuddling your child or dog/cat. Giving unexpected hugs are great ways to relax.
- Centering on the positive things in your life. It is essential to begin affirmations and focus on the positive traits you have as a *good person.* Use the following journal page to start and continue as you work to resolve your grief.

Journal Entry

Date:

Write the following or your own positive affirmation:

I am a good person with only pure intentions. I am lovable and loving, dependable and love myself as I am. Fill this page!

Journal Entry

Date:

Strategies Chosen:

Relaxation Techniques Chosen:

Thoughts: (What are you thinking?)

Other Strategies

A relationship review begins when you are able to talk about your experience. Start telling your story. Ask your friend, or a therapist to listen. This is one of the most important components of stage I, when grieving a living loss.

It is essential to remain with your feelings until a review of the lost relationship is completed. This may take time. More than one telling will be necessary. To lessen the difficulty with your life review, show family pictures, including the enforcer and family members. Shock, sadness and deep pain are still present in this stage. You may experience guilt, self blame, and confusion. Possibly angry feelings may also be expressed.

Journal writing is especially helpful. **Buy your journal now!!** Later on, journal pages are provided for you to do specific writings, as well as a place to note feelings and thinking about certain things. Initially, journal entries such as your relationship review, "feelings letters" and structured writings tend to be very long.

Structured journal writing helps you to get started. You choose to answer a specific question or write about a certain topic that seems to be difficult. To start the process, set a timer for ten minutes and commit to writing for that length of time. Remember this is only to get you started, you may write as long as you wish. You need to eventually see the positives and negatives of the relationship. It is necessary for the grieving person to see the ***complete picture*** of interaction between the estranged family members. This process takes time, and is sometimes difficult.

Further strategies can be developed by:

- Initiating a discussion with an immediate family member (son, daughter, partner) and/or a friend. You need to find support. Try to verbalize what your needs are. Explore what changes can be made in order to help the grieving process.
- Answering the following question in your journal:

What changes do I need to make to help myself the most?

Working on changing your thoughts and setting boundaries is necessary. To do this, try to limit the time spent thinking about the negativity of the situation. Each day, when you awaken, observe your thoughts. If your first thought is about the enforcer, tell yourself; "I will not think these thoughts for one hour". You will not ***stop*** the thoughts but you will ***interrupt*** them. Gradually, you can extend the hour to two hours and so on until you are able to extinguish these thoughts almost completely.

As the estranged person, you may still be in **shock** when you say, "I can't believe that this has happened" or "I don't know what to say". Grief is still very active and deep. Emotions of grief may spiral when discussing the enforcer and the situation. There is a strong need to share the experience of not having had anyone to talk to. Making a comment such as "I don't really care", may conflict with "I can't bear to hear the name without crying". The feelings are very much that of the victim as well as being conflicted.

Listening is very important in this process. The story needs to be told over and over again, in therapy, as well as outside, with supportive people. The grieving person has probably felt a self imposed ***silence*** for a very long time. It is time to begin exploring the relationship. Look at what ***you can do*** rather than ***what has been done to you.***

Journal Entry

Date:

Write the following or your own positive affirmation:

I am a good person with only pure intentions. I am lovable and loving, dependable and love myself as I am. Fill this page!

Journal Entry

Date:

Structured Journal Writing:

Journal writing is helpful especially when it is *structured as described previously.*

Relationship Review: (Write your relationship story here or in your personal journal, it may be very long).

Things you can do: The suggestion of writing a *"feelings" letter* will be repeated several times throughout the book. This is an individual healing process that may be done at any time either on your journal page or in the private journal you have purchased. It is not meant to be mailed. You will date your letters and keep them to be read later, at the end of your healing journey.

- Write a "feelings" letter to the enforcer with no intention of mailing it. ***This is an expression of feelings experienced during the isolation and initial shock of estrangement.*** In the beginning, it may be very long.
- Dedicate time to journal writing. If you have difficulty beginning your entry, you may wish to use *structured journal writing.* Set a timer and write for at least ten minutes about your experience using the *observer perception.* That is, stepping back, and being detached from the situation. Talk about your grief and your role within the family.

It is time to observe your feelings:

- your preoccupation with memories of the enforcer and the family members
- your deep pain, and sadness which often causes crying
- your painful path of doubt and uncertainty of self
- your guilt and self blame
- your confusion

At this point, when *confusion* sets in you are giving in to:

- feeling terribly wronged
- feeling guilty
- feeling responsible
- feeling betrayed
- experiencing triggers

Tracing the past:

Throughout the first part of your healing journey you have begun to face the past as an enforced person. It is now time to face, trace and erase the pain.

- ***FACE*** (write about your past relationship experience with the enforcer).
- ***TRACE*** (bring to mind the pain you are feeling as you are writing).
- ***ERASE*** (practice cognitive mental devices, and relaxation strategies you have learned in order to release that pain).

You may be thinking about:

- always having to think the same as my family
- not expressing my thoughts and feelings in order to belong
- there is never any *real* communication
- not being able to express my own needs
- the relationship with the enforcer has often been painful
- starting to set boundaries and disengaging from the relationship
- feelings of hopelessness, helplessness and disrespect
- reacting negatively when excluded from family events and family communications
- being perceived as a difficult person, in the eyes of the enforcer
- sensing that there will always be a form of exclusion

Journal Entry

Date:

Answer the following questions:

What changes do I need to make to help myself the most?

What am I thinking and feeling?

Journal Entry

Date:

Write about what you can do rather than what has been done to you.

What am I thinking and feeling?

Journal Entry

Date:

Tracing the past:

- ***FACE*** (write about your past relationship experience with the enforcer).
- ***TRACE*** (bring to mind the pain you are feeling as you are writing).
- ***ERASE*** (practice cognitive mental devices, and relaxation strategies you have learned in order to release(that pain).

Journal Entry

Date:

Write a "**feelings**" **letter** to the enforcer with no intention of mailing it. You may wish to write in your personal journal, it could be very long. Date each letter for reading at the end of your healing journey. If you have difficulty beginning your entry, you may wish to use ***structured journal writing. Use observer perception.*** That is, stepping back, and being detached from the situation. Talk about your grief and your role within the family.

Therapeutic Pathways

There are numerous healing approaches such as bio energy therapy, emotional freedom techniques (EMF), reality therapy (RT) and so on. My approach is a 'diverse mix' of therapeutic tools. However, since I am certified in choice theory/reality therapy, I present various RT strategies throughout your healing journey with me. I feel these tools provide a successful way for you to take charge of your own healing. You can make a conscious choice to change your thinking as you work through your grief.

Reality therapy focuses on teaching people to fulfill the need of being loved and loving, and the need of feeling worthwhile to oneself and others. Dr. Glasser believes that people learn to do this through:

- **Reality**, defined as the willingness to accept the consequences of our behavior.
- **Responsibility**, defined as the ability to meet our needs without infringing on others' rights to meet their needs.
- **Right and Wrong**, defined as something you know by how you feel.
- **Behaviour,** defined as what we use to satisfy our needs. Behaviour is chosen. We can only change our own behavior, not that of other people.
- ***Total behaviour*** consists of four components, thinking, acting, feeling and physiology or bodily functioning.

Your journey becomes less difficult when you are able to understand what you want and what you can do. By making better choices you learn to meet your own needs. You learn to use the RT questions, found throughout this book, and apply them to your grief resolution. The bibliography includes books you may choose to read.

As noted, Dr. William Glasser developed choice theory which is at the core of reality therapy (RT). He sees the indicators of emotional problems as the result of the inability to fulfill one's basic needs.

This approach is not just for therapists. You can register for Basic Intensive in Choice Theory and Reality Therapy training, in order to expand your self-development journey or using the bibliography, read more about choice theory/reality therapy. By learning important strategies, you will be better equipped to meet with crises throughout your life time. Making the choice to attend the initial workshop has been a turning point for many people.

Dr. Glasser believes that there is a connection between lack of success in meeting needs and the degree of distress experienced often indicated by core distress symptoms.

Core Distress Symptoms

Sleeplessness
Confusion
Lack of concentration
Anger
Physical symptoms
Change in appetite (eating more or less)
Sadness
Others______________________

- Record these scores and date on the following journal pages.

You are now beginning to heal. The rest of your healing journey consists of gaining information, as well as using helpful strategies and techniques for each stage of your healing.

This is a **turning point**. At this time you need to look at the **'whole picture'.** You can do this by asking and answering reality therapy questions on the following journal pages:

- **What do I want?**
- **What am I doing to get what I want?**
- **Is it working?**
- **If not, what can I do differently?**
- **What is my plan?**

Journal Entry

Date:

- Sleeplessness

  ____

- Confusion

  ____

- Lack of concentration

  ____

- Anger

  ____

- Physical symptoms

  ____

- Change in appetite (eating more or less)

  ____

- Sadness

  ____

- Others

  ____

Thoughts: (What you are thinking?)

Journal Entry

Date:

Answer the following questions:

What do I want?

What am I doing to get what I want?

Is it working?

If not, what can I do differently?

What is my plan?

You may wish to use structured writing in your personal journal at this time. Extra journal sheets are provided for you at the end of the book. Always evaluate your plan from time to time.

Possible Experiences Along the Way:

Check any of the following statements you have experienced.

___Realizing that compromise of self was evident before the estrangement

___The inability to express thoughts and feelings about your experience

___The development of serious health problems

___Feeling responsible for the negative family involvement

___Experiencing mental exhaustion and burnout

___Racing thoughts and attempting to process **Why did this happen to me?**

___Constantly asking **Why do I have no support from family members?**

___Little or no sharing of loss experience with friends or professionals

___Experiencing strong triggers that set off deep pain and constant reminders of loss

___Feeling betrayed by the enforcer and family members

___Endless struggling with the conflict of wanting to feel loved and included in the family circle and the fear that nothing is changing

___Very little acknowledgement of your pain and loss by family members

___Feeling that the door for any further discussion is closed

___Feeling that family members seem to have aligned with the enforcer

___Feelings of loss and helplessness. The need for love and belonging is not met.

___Body, mind and spirit have been negatively affected

___The role of victim has become entrenched into your being

___Having feelings of disbelief, shock and being in crisis mode

___Any attempt to contact the enforcer is rejected

___Seeking therapy to alleviate stress/burnout, anxiety, depression, sleep difficulties, and other symptoms

___The possibility that the focus is on the above stress symptoms and not the estrangement from a close family member

___Continuing to feel engulfed by the grief of this loss

Choose YOUR most difficult experiences by circling some of the previous check marks.

Journal Entry

Date:

Write about YOUR most difficult experiences – the circled check marks from preceding page.

You may need to use your personal journal.

Journal Entry

Date:

Write the following or your own positive affirmation:

I am a good person with only pure intentions. I am lovable and loving, dependable and love myself as I am. Fill this page!

Think about **what you have learned**. You have reached out to another person. This may be a friend or a therapist. At this point, in your healing journey you are,

- Beginning the habit of doing your journal pages
- Understanding structured journal writing when these feelings are blocked
- ***Talking*** about your experiences with a special family member, friend or therapist ***is a very important step***
- Contemplating any questions you may have, or other questions as they appear throughout the rest of this book.
- Addressing the **Possible Experiences Statements** you previously chose to be your most difficult experiences by circling some of the check marks in the exercise.

There is a powerful need in human beings to be **validated**. Telling your story gives you the validation and affirmation you desire. Initiate this by saying to your friend or therapist, ***I need you to listen to my story. I may have to tell it many times.***

There needs to be a **release of emotions**. Understand that an emotional ***break down*** may surface. Unresolved feelings such as anger, or sadness, may occur. Feelings of shock and disbelief will continue. These emotions need to be experienced.

What happens at this time is okay. This is the beginning. If you become overwhelmed with emotions, stop. Focus on your breath while doing abdominal breathing, listen to relaxation music, or practice relaxation through visualization.

Using these strategies and in your own time, you will realize that you are ***no longer the victim. When you take responsibility for yourself , you make progress, and your self esteem increases.***

- You are no longer the victim when you take responsibility for your own healing.
- Through ***doing***, you will feel a shift. Perhaps you are feeling lighter, or that a burden is lifting from your shoulders.

"ACTION" Strategies

It is time to:

- **Change your thinking and begin 'doing'**
- **If you haven't already done so, purchase a personal journal for longer writings**
- **Use journal pages found in this book**

Begin with the affirmation: ***I have what it takes to resolve my loss.*** Use these positive words when negativity takes over your thinking. Writing these words over and over will help to make healing pathways. Set your immediate goals. As noted, you may use your core distress symptoms to do so. For example, I want to sleep better, or be more active. I want to cry less and feel hopeful. I want to be less angry.

- **Relaxation strategies** are important at this time.
- **Practice mindful deep breathing, relaxation exercises and visualization techniques.**
- The ***story, or relationship review,*** is an important component in the resolution of a living loss. Talking about your experience and remaining with your feelings until the journey of reviewing this broken relationship is complete, will be extremely helpful.
- It is important to ***focus on yourself.*** Find time to return to an enjoyable interest, or start a new one, such as knitting, sewing, drawing, painting, gardening, or singing. It is time to start a daily exercise regime. Often it is difficult to start. Try telling yourself that you will walk 10 minutes from your house and return. Or try other activities like hiking, chopping wood, dancing, doing a structured work-out. You will produce endorphins which elevate your positive mood.
- Reading reality therapy books suggested in the bibliography will give you insight into your own needs and strengths. Choosing from these and other books will help you to further understand the depth of your journey (using the internet may be more helpful when researching topics such as social taboos, socialization of families). Use extra journal pages, if necessary.
- Explore social taboos, myths and family rules. How do they affect me?

- What is a co-dependent family? Do I have one?
- What are my personal needs, how do they differ from those of other family members?
- How can I assess the strengths of my own needs?
- What relaxation techniques can I use?
- What is the picture in my mind of my lost relationship?
- What are my needs and strengths?

The rest of your healing journey consists of valuable information learned along the way with helpful strategies for each stage of your healing. Please continue.

Journal Entry

Date:

Affirmations: You may wish to use your personal journal.

Write all affirmations often:

- **I am no longer the victim.**
- **I have what it takes to resolve my loss.**

Journal Entry

Date:

Set your immediate goals. You may use your core distress symptoms to do so. For example, I want to sleep better, or be more active. I want to cry less and feel hopeful. I want to be less angry.

Journal Entry

Date:

Write a "**feelings**" **letter** to the enforcer with no intention of mailing it. You may wish to write in your personal journal, it may be very long. Date each letter, for reading at the end of your healing journey. If you have difficulty beginning your entry, you may wish to use ***structured journal writing. Use observer perception***. That is, stepping back, and being detached from the situation. Talk about your grief and your role within the family.

Journal Entry

Date:

Write the following or your own positive affirmation:

I am a good person with only pure intentions. I am lovable and loving, dependable and love myself as I am. Fill this page!

Journal Entry

Date:

Write the affirmation: I have what it takes to resolve my loss. Focus on what you are writing. Fill the page!

Journal Entry

Date:

Again, ask yourself reality therapy questions:

What do I want?

What am I doing to get what I want?

Is it working?

If it is not working, what can I do differently? (My plan) You may wish to use structured journal writing at this time. Extra journal sheets are provided for you at the end of the book. **Evaluate your plan often.**

Journal Entry

Date:

What are you thinking?

Journal Entry

Date:

Answer these questions (you may wish to use your personal journal):

What are social taboos, myths and family rules. How do they affect me?

What is a co-dependent family? Do I have one?

What are my personal needs, how do they differ from those of other family members?

How can I assess the strengths of my own needs?

What relaxation techniques can I use?

What is the picture in my mind of my lost relationship?

Journal Entry

Date:

As you have done previously, write a **"feelings" letter** to the enforcer. These are reminders, you can write this letter at any time. You may wish to jot down a few notes here before ***dating*** and writing the letter in your personal journal. You will read them at the end of your healing journey.

Journal Entry

Date:

What are my needs and strengths?

Can I change the relationship picture I have in my mind?

Can I change the picture of me and my loved one as two human beings who are not perfect?

Can I change the ideal or perfect picture to the realities of the situation I am in?

Thoughts: (What am I thinking?)

Remaining in the Present Strategies

The strategies which follow will help you to **remain in the present.** Periodically, throughout the day, ask yourself:

At this moment ....
What am I doing??
What am I thinking??
What am I feeling??
How am I breathing??

In the beginning you may have better success in remembering to ask these questions, if you set your watch, or computer, at regular intervals during the day or use turning on a light switch, or opening a desk drawer as a reminder.

Before you read about and put into practice the strategies for stage II grieving, there are **others** you may choose to do.

If possible, continue discussing your painful journey with a supportive immediate family member who may be willing to listen. It is possible that some family members did not discuss the estrangement with you, fearing the pain and sadness that would surface. Dialogue with them about how you feel.

- You may wish to read some of your journal pages, or focus on your goals.
- Again, you might need to go through family pictures that include the enforcer, and other extended family members.
- It may be helpful to keep these pictures. You can make an album for viewing, when the loss is resolved.

Cognitive Strategies

Cognitive or thinking strategies will allow you to remain in the present. You become the observer of your own thoughts. Set **boundaries** for these thoughts. For example:

- Tell yourself that you will not think about the enforcer for one hour (as noted previously).
- Extend the time as you resolve your grief (two hours, three hours).
- It will take some time before the ***thought stopping*** takes place.
- In the beginning, you will first interrupt your compulsive thoughts of the enforcer.
- Eventually the length of time between them will become longer.

You are still in shock if you find yourself saying:

I can't quite accept that this has happened.
I can't really think what to say about the relationship.
I can't believe he/she would do this.

Shock is still very much evident in these statements.

It is time to **switch gears** as we enter stage two,

- Begin to explore the relationship omitting the idea of ***What has been done to me?***
- Place the focus on ***What can I do?***

Continue with the following:

- Write another ***feelings letter*** to the enforcer. Remember this is not a letter you will send.
- Throughout the journey of resolving your loss, you will write this letter several times. As the feelings change, the letter will change.
- Keep these letters in a safe place, only for re-reading later in your healing. In a future ritual, you can read them in order and then burn them.

Journal Entry

Date:

Write the following or your own positive affirmation:

I am a good person with only pure intentions. I am lovable and loving, dependable and love myself as I am. Fill this page!

Scaling your Progress

Again, **Core distress symptoms** indicate your response to grieving.

Express what you are feeling and experiencing through your journal.

Write about what is happening to your body, as well as what you are thinking. Review your progress. At this time, use your journal pages to ***review and record your distress symptoms*** which may be some, or all, of the following:

Sleeplessness
Confusion
Lack of concentration
Anger
Physical symptoms
Change in appetite (eating more or less)
Sadness
Others________________________

Record these scores and date on your journal page which follows.

Journal Entry

Date:

Use scaling (1 – 10) and review your progress. At this time, use your journal to review and record your distress symptoms which may be some or all of the following:

- Sleeplessness

  ____

- Confusion

  ____

- Lack of concentration

  ____

- Anger

  ____

- Physical symptoms

  ____

- Change in appetite (eating more or less)

  ____

- Sadness

  ____

- Others

  ____

Journal Entry

Date:

Write another "feelings" letter to the enforcer. This is not a letter you will send. Keep these letters in a safe place, only for re-reading later in your healing. In a future ritual, you can read them in order and then burn them.

Journal Entry

Date:

Express what you are feeling and experiencing through your journal. Write about what is happening to your body, as well as what you are thinking.

Journal Entry

Date:

Write the following or your own positive affirmation:

I am a good person with only pure intentions. I am lovable and loving, dependable and love myself as I am. Fill this page!

Chapter IX

Changing Our Thinking: Grieving Stage II

"Life is not your enemy, but thinking can be".
Wayne Dwyer

This is the acute stage. It is most often filled with anger toward the offending person. The grieving person has been unable to say loud and clear that this situation is *not* fair. Usually the enforced is filled with unbridled anger, and adamant that the situation is not his/her fault. Total blame is directed to the enforcer.

Every mean and nasty act that has ever been ***perceived by the enforced person*** dominates thinking. Remember that your ***perception of events changes*** as you resolve the grief of a living loss. As you heal, your perception will be different. It is necessary to work with how you feel and think in each stage of grief. This behaviour is contrary to the first stage, when, as the wounded person (the enforced) you had taken the blame and responsibility for the relationship breakup.

When it is realized that the estrangement is probably not temporary, the anger becomes deep-seated. The grieving person may become a martyr, wallowing in self pity when regarding the enforcer.

The triggers will remain, since the processing of anger has mostly occurred in the person's mind. There seems to be progress until the estranged person hears a story about the family, or remembers some involvement. Memories, either positive or negative, now seem better than no contact at all. There is a deep feeling of confusion and not knowing which way to turn. At this time, it is important to recognize and resolve the conflicts you are feeling.

Addressing Conflict #1:

The first conflict sets in: The feelings of ***still wanting to be a part of the family and feeling deep anger toward them.*** Unfortunately the skills for negotiation and compromising necessary to resolve a conflict are absent when there is no contact with the enforcer.

The situation continues to feel hopeless. Although somewhat stronger, the alienated person is still experiencing a lack of support when attempting to verbalize feelings with another family member. It is a very difficult time.

During this time certain family members may deliver short messages that the estrangement has gone on long enough. A family courier, might ask directly if the grieving person wants to renew the relationship with the enforcer. Your reaction, as the bereaved person could be one of shock.

You may have ***felt*** that most family members were aligned with the enforcer and this validates that they actually are. As noted previously, you will feel differently at the end of your healing journey. ***It is necessary to deal with your feelings and thinking at this time.*** The reminder of betrayal and rejection magnifies the remorse. Negative body symptoms such as the inability to sleep, the lack of concentration and headaches may appear.

Journal Entry

Date:

Conflict # 1

Write about the feelings of still wanting to be a part of the family and feeling deep anger toward them.

Your confusion and vulnerable state of mind may cause you to act negatively toward the messenger. Because of your anger toward the person who enforced the situation, your response will not likely be positive. You might indicate that the possibility of having a relationship does not exist. Fear takes over. Feeling hopeless and helpless, the perception sets in that the last chance to be admitted back to the family has been lost. Long term pain may resurface and intensify.

The negative reaction is often a true reflection of the uncertain, stressed, and anxious state of the grieving person. There are feelings of not knowing what the ***truth*** is. Whatever the truth is, rejecting the offer could mean that it will be quickly withdrawn by the enforcer.

A difficult situation such as this can be seen as an ***opportunity*** and not a crisis. Whether or not the preceding scenario has occurred, it is time to work on further strategies. You, the enforced person, may now choose to continue processing the pain and grief that is still present.

It is necessary to ***decide*** what you need from the lost relationship, or, if it is wanted at all. When you are able to respond without reacting emotionally and negatively, it is time to move on. A door has truly been opened for you.

Strategies are important. It is now time to reframe your perspective, as the grieving person, and grasp the idea of formulating a goal. Ask yourself the following questions:

What is it I want?, What am I going to do, to get what I want?

- It is time to explore another truth of the estrangement. Consider life with and without the enforcer.
- Explore the feelings of shame, guilt, self blame. Acknowledge family myths and rules, and the lack of support. Seek validation from your friend or therapist. You have probably been silent a long time.

Consider the purpose of this long and painful journey. When you are validated and supported, you will feel stronger emotionally. You are ready to accept the idea that the relationship has been toxic. ***The***

feelings of disrespect and disconnection are not your own neurotic thoughts. They exist.

You are again at a turning-point.

As the grieving person, you can now respond to future possibilities. Changes can be made.

Consider new and different philosophies regarding life's journey. Explore new thinking such as We attract what we fear. When one door closes, another one opens. I am going to look at this experience as an opportunity and not a crisis. What am I to learn from this?

Journal Entry

Date:

Write the following or your own positive affirmation:

I am a good person with only pure intentions. I am lovable and loving, dependable and love myself as I am. Fill this page!

Journal Entry

Date:

Write About:

We attract what we fear. When one door closes, another one opens. I am going to look at this experience as an opportunity and not a crisis. What am I to learn from this?

Journal Entry

Date:

Write a **"feelings" letter** to the person with no intention of mailing it.

Check the bibliography. Choosing to read some of these books will assist you in continuing to grow and develop through further learning.

At this time it is likely that you are somewhat stronger emotionally than previously and can think more clearly.

Open your mind to the idea that you can love someone and be unable to have a relationship with him or her. You may continue to love in a spiritual way, and even extend wishes for a good life.

- Interaction is beyond your reach but loving is possible
- There are two people in a relationship Both need to make changes
- Ask yourself "In a family that lacks communication skills, could both persons be at fault for the break-up?"

Resolving anger:

If your anger seems to be overwhelming, work with it appropriately. Structured journalizing, regarding your anger, may be healing at this time. Continue dialoguing about anger with your friend or therapist. Use relaxation techniques.

You may need to take the opportunity to **state your anger as below or with other words.** Loudly and clearly say:

WHAT HAPPENED IS NOT MY FAULT.
THIS ESTRANGEMENT IS NOT FAIR.

If this is the way you feel, at this time, record the words, or similar words, in your journal on the next page. Do structured writing beginning with the above statements. Write about your anger. Talk about your anger with someone you trust.

Victimization, self pity and martyrdom may exist at this point.

Journal Entry

Date:

Write about: Resolving anger. This could be a long entry for your personal journal. You may need to do this several times - state your anger as below or with other words, loudly and clearly:

WHAT HAPPENED IS NOT MY FAULT.
THIS ESTRANGEMENT IS NOT FAIR.

Continue reflective journaling and thinking by:

- recalling negative acts of the enforcer that dominate your thinking.
- being aware of feelings of confusion about the self-blame and the responsibility you feel.
- realizing that estrangement may be permanent.
- experiencing continued deep anger.
- writing about deep anger.

Your progress is in a state of change:

- you may have regressed back to past thoughts and behaviours.
- fear is knocking at your door.
- you feel you have lost the chance for a relationship.
- triggers remain.
- conflicts begin to seep into your consciousness.

Journal Entry

Date:

Write about: Negative acts of the enforcer that dominate your thinking. This could be a long entry for your personal journal. You may need to do this several times.

- **Being aware of feelings of confusion about the self-blame and responsibility you feel.**
- **Realizing that estrangement may be permanent.**
- **Experiencing continued deep anger.**

Journal Entry

Date:

Write the following or your own positive affirmation:

I am a good person with only pure intentions. I am lovable and loving, dependable and love myself as I am. Fill this page!

You are still trying to resolve conflict #1:

You want to be part of the family, including the enforcer's and other family members' lives. At the same time you fear reconnection.

There has been:

- no ***further*** contact
- no negotiation or compromise.
- a feeling of helplessness and hopelessness
- a lack of success when approaching key family members
- a sense of betrayal from family members
- a feeling of being responsible for the estrangement

Checking in – The picture at present

Record Core Distress Symptoms

Using your journal, document ***what you are experiencing now. Where are you on a scale of one to ten?***

Sleeplessness
Lack of concentration
Anger
Physical symptoms
Change in appetite (eating more or less)
Sadness
Others______________________

Date and record the answers on the following journal page. As well, enter ***what you are thinking and feeling at this time.***

Journal Entry

Date:

Use scaling (1 – 10) and review your progress. At this time, use your journal to review and record your distress symptoms which may be some or all of the following:

- Sleeplessness

  ____

- Confusion

  ____

- Lack of concentration

  ____

- Anger

  ____

- Physical symptoms

  ____

- Change in appetite (eating more or less)

  ____

- Sadness

  ____

- Others

  ____

Write Here

There are different scenarios for different people:

- the enforcer has not, and seemingly will not, contact you
- the enforcer contacts you through a family messenger stating that there needs to be an end to the estrangement
- you react negatively
- you meet the enforcer at a family gathering
- there is no apology or conversation regarding the estrangement
- you hear from a family member that according to the enforcer, there is nothing to talk about
- the enforcer was angry and now wants the estrangement over
- you want better communication with the enforcer
- you need assurance that there will be a change in the relationship
- the reality of family betrayal is clear as the messages are related by family members
- lack of trust is a major issue

Regardless of where you are in the scenario, you are ***VULNERABLE*** and still filled with shock.

Confusion, Shock and Anger

There exists a very negative climate. You must decide if you can accept the relationship without discussing the problems that exist between you and the enforcer. At this point, your mental and emotional strength have increased and you are probably stronger than the fear you feel. It is time to state over and over that you will not be ***driven*** by your emotions. When you experience a trigger, you can acknowledge its presence without a strong negative reaction. That is, you experience a trigger and acknowledge what it is. You feel strong as you change your thinking to ***I will not allow my thinking to be manipulated.***

Journal Entry

Date:

Affirmation:

I will not be driven by my emotions.

Journal Entry

Date:

Write another "feelings" letter to the enforcer. You may wish to make a few notes here and write the letter in your personal journal. Remember to record the date for reading at the end of your journey.

It is time to return to the present:

Now is the time to formulate long term goals. In your journal, answer these important questions:

1. ***What do I want?***
2. ***Is it necessary for the lost relationship to continue?***
3. ***What am I doing to get what I want?***

State what you want from a relationship with the enforcer (what are your goals):

____

____

____

____

____

____

____

____

____

____

____

____

____

If it is difficult to formulate these goals, use the previous questions to do structured writing in your journal as you have done previously. Again use the affirmation - I will no longer be driven by my emotions.

Journal Entry

Date:

Write About:

1. **What do I want?**
2. **Is it necessary for the lost relationship to continue?**
3. **What am I doing to get what I want (plan)?**

Restate more fully what you want from a relationship with the enforcer. Evaluate your plan.

You are now at a more **cognitive,** or thinking level. It is time to understand the shame, guilt, and self blame you have experienced. As well, you need to explore further reading, in order to understand the influence of family norms, myths, or rules, the lack of support of an important family member, and the lack of communication in the family. Some suggestions are in the bibliography.

Through reading, you will receive further validation of the effect family dynamics have had on you as a member of the family.

Three important questions, only you can answer:

- How is my thinking different now than from the beginning of my journey.
- What could have been the purpose of this long and painful journey?
- What have I learned?

Answer these questions through structured journal writing.

It is quite probable that you have grown emotionally. ***Now you are strong enough not only to consider, but to believe the following:***

- the relationship had been toxic for a long time
- a lack of direct and honest communication has occurred often within the family
- feelings of disrespect and disconnection were not neurotic – they existed
- it is possible to visualize new hope for the future with or without the enforcer.

Explore **changes in your thinking.** ***You may have to expand your perception of the truth.*** Remember, we all perceive events differently. Eventually you will have enough distance and be strong enough to better understand the enforcer.

At this time, ***you can consider future possibilities and make changes. It is time to internalize what you have learned***. That is, choose what will become part of your own belief system regarding:

- family myths and rules
- co-dependent families
- new philosophies regarding your life journey

Journal Entry

Date:

Written Affirmation:

I will no longer be driven by my emotions.

Journal Entry

Date:

Three important questions, only you can answer:

- How is my thinking different now than from the beginning of my journey?
- What could have been the purpose of this long and painful journey?
- What have I learned?

Journal Entry

Date:

Write the following or your own positive affirmation:

I am a good person with only pure intentions. I am lovable and loving, dependable and love myself as I am. Fill this page!

You are thinking more clearly now. Intellectually you already understand these new ideas. You are ready to begin practising internalizing the following statements until they are part of your belief system:

- I can love someone and **be unable** to have a relationship.
- I can love spiritually and not interact personally.
- Both adults are responsible for the estrangement.

This is a check point. It is time for further examination of self.

How are **your** own communication skills, assertiveness and interaction with ***your entire family?*** It is quite likely that you can communicate very well outside the family. If not, you may wish to take an assertiveness training course. Do not confuse assertiveness with aggressiveness. Read about communication and/or take a course.

Write in your journal about your remaining anger. It is time to write another "feelings" letter with no intention of mailing it. Daily affirm the following statement or one similar. Repeat and write this affirmation often.

I have what it takes to detach from this anger.

Journal Entry

Date:

You may wish to write another feelings letter, either here or in your personal journal.

Journal Entry

Date:

Write the following affirmation many times. Think about what you are writing.

I have what it takes to detach from my anger.

Chapter X

Moving on: Grieving Stage III

"You will never grow until you take some steps outside your comfort zone".
Hal Urban

It is now time for resolution, acceptance and moving forward. Reintegration into social situations with the family may or may not be possible. If possible, it will be easier through the strength gained from your journey of healing. As the estranged person, you may be ready to clearly focus on the ***whole picture*** of the estrangement. Perhaps you are feeling that it is time for self examination and removing the focus from the other person.

Addressing Conflict #2

A decision is ***essential*** in order to continue healing. The **second conflict** needs to be addressed. If there has been no further verbal contact with the enforcer you are probably:

- wanting to return to the relationship and feeling that no verbal communication with the enforcer means nothing is likely to change.

Answer the following questions on the next journal page:

- Is it probable that I have wanted more love than is possible for that person to give?
- Is it possible for me to continue living on the fringe of the relationship?

Think about the answers. Write them here or in your personal journal.

Journal Entry

Date:

Addressing Conflict #2

Write about the following, either here or in your personal journal:

- Is it probable that I have wanted more love than is possible for that person to give?
- Is it possible for me to continue living on the fringe of the relationship?

Are you feeling that it is time for self examination and removing the focus from the other person?

It is now time for ***further self-examination*** as you visualize a future relationship with the enforcer. Answer ***yes or no*** to the following questions. This will expand your self-understanding.

____Will I feel equal in this relationship?

____Will I express myself truthfully and naturally?

____Will I feel accepted?

____Will I feel safe and secure?

____Can I trust again?

____Can I re-enter the lost relationship with no verbal exchange or communication?

____Would anything be different in the relationship without a discussion with the enforcer?

____Will I feel comfortable, if the relationship remains the same?

____Am I still driven by triggers of the living loss (emotionally)?

If the answer is **NO** to each question, or **the majority of the questions**, it would seem that the relationship remains toxic for you, as a grieving person. At this time only you can honestly answer these questions which will periodically rise throughout your self development.

Further questions to consider are:

- How do I achieve my needs at this time?
- Is it possible to get what I want in the relationship?

It is extremely important to know what it is ***you*** want. From what you have learned so far, you should be able to answer the previous questions.

It is sometimes difficult because the answer may not be what we want to hear. If this is an uncomfortable issue for you, return to structured journal writing of these two questions or discuss them with your friend or therapist. Extra journal sheets are provided for you at the end of the book.

Journal Entry

Date:

Write the following or your own positive affirmation:

I am a good person with only pure intentions. I am lovable and loving, dependable and love myself as I am. Fill this page!

Journal Entry

Date:

Write here or in your personal journal:

- How do I achieve my needs at this time?
- Is it possible to get what I want in the relationship?

Journal Entry

Date:

Take the ***time*** to recognize your progress. On a scale of 1 – 10 - What is your score? Look at the ***"whole picture"*** of your **healing ______.**

Record Core Distress Symptoms (scaling as above). Compare it with the first scaling scores.

- Sleeplessness

  ____
- Confusion

  ____
- Lack of concentration

  ____
- Anger

  ____
- Physical symptoms

  ____
- Change in appetite (eating more or less)

  ____
- Sadness

  ____
- Others

  ____

If your scores have not increased considerably from previous scaling, it is necessary for you to do further grief resolution work. Make a commitment to do relaxation techniques, choose a hobby or interest, increase activity, etc. You may also benefit from seeing your physician and a therapist.

You are opening the door to progress through:

- making your own decisions
- making changes in your thoughts and actions

Strategies

Decision-making and making changes are necessary at this time. Discuss the following options and perceptions with your friend or therapist. Although you have previously considered these questions, you need to record them in your journal.

Is it possible that I am wanting more love than the other person can give?

Is it possible for me to continue living on the fringe of this relationship with no change in behavour or communication with the enforcer?

Remain conscious of these two questions throughout the rest of your journey. When you feel stuck, return to what you have written previously. Evaluate what you have written and write again.

Decision Making Strategies:

Please note that the following strategies are meant to be a private exploration of relationship possibilities with the enforcer. They are not appropriate for online conversation:

- Set personal boundaries. Let the enforcer know that you are open to a discussion regarding a possible relationship.
- Decide how you will be available in order to explore reconnecting. Will you make a personal visit? Will you telephone, or write a letter?
- Define for yourself what it is that you want in the relationship before you make any contact. This may be a written exercise. You may want to use the structured journal writing process.
- Consider that through this journey, you have become a stronger, less needy person who does not need to be loved by everyone. You are open to an adult relationship based on communication, respect and equality. You will try to make contact. The next step is up to the enforcer. It is his/her choice.
- If you make contact, arrange for a meeting. The parameters of your adult relationship with the enforcer need to be set verbally. Perhaps if a relationship is not deemed possible, there could be an exchange of cards or another type of annual contact.

Journal Entry

Date:

Write about:

Is it possible that I am wanting more love than the other person can give?

Is it possible for me to continue living on the fringe of this relationship with no change in behaviour or communication with the enforcer?

There are certain things you need to think about:

- Will returning to the relationship mean too much compromising on my part? Can I be myself in a relationship with this person?
- How do I feel when I meet this person? (Do I still feel uncomfortable? The situation may still be ***toxic*** for you.)
- Do I still feel a deep need to have a relationship? (Perhaps with your new emotional growth you have no vision of ever being close to this person.)
- Consider that it may not be possible to have a relationship with this person.
- Can I honestly wish this person only the best from my heart, without having a relationship? (Remember you can love someone and not like their behaviours.)
- Can I continue to compromise myself in this relationship?

What is your situation regarding the relationship at present? Do you relate to any of the following scripts?

- Re-connection is a possibility. The offer to reunite came through a family member. There has been no communication with the enforcer. There is little indication that anything has changed. This could be a "patch up" job in which you will be expected to play the same role. The chance of reinstatement on shared terms seems quite unlikely.
- You have met the person at a family gathering. There was no hint of any estrangement or disconnection. You enjoyed the company of the enforcer.
- You received a second message from a family member. The enforcer had stated; "It was nothing. I got mad. That's it." There appears to be denial on the part of the enforcer in a very clear and definite way.

Are you making progress?

Things are likely to be more clear now.

There is a dawning of understanding that both persons in this situation need to make changes in order to have a positive relationship.

A lifetime of learning to process this loss is apparent.

A huge step has been taken in the realization that life is not always fair. You don't always get what you want but you can change your response and move on.

Remaining in the present allows you to focus on all the loving and positive people in your life.

You are a fully developed adult. Your emotional strength allows you to have a casual relationship with the enforcer. You can wish this person well in the future.

Your anger is depleted. Your heart is open.

There is hope at the end of this journey.

You can visualize life with or without the enforcer.

If you disagree with some of these statements, write in your personal journal or on the next journal page. Write about your feelings.

Journal Entry

Date:

If things still seem to be unclear, and you disagree with some of these statements, write them down.

Go back to your personal journal and do structured writing about how you feel at this time. Continue your journey whether or not you feel stuck. Perhaps relaxation techniques need to be increased.

Realism

It is again time to use your reality therapy equation:

What do I want?

What am I doing to get what I want?

Is it working?

- **Evaluate:** What is your decision? Can you return to this relationship?

It is up to you to answer these questions. You may wish to use structured journal writing at this time. Perhaps you would prefer to discuss the decision-making process with your friend or therapist.

Journal Entry

Date:

Write About: Realism. Remember, when you find yourself writing in depth, go to your personal journal.

What do I want?

What am I doing to get what I want?

Is it working?

Can I plan to return to the relationship?

Evaluate your plan.

Journal Entry

Date:

Look at the ***"whole picture"*** of your healing. On a scale of 1 – 10 record your score below:

____

Record Core Distress Symptoms (scaling as above)

- Sleeplessness

  ____

- Confusion

  ____

- Lack of concentration

  ____

- Anger

  ____

- Physical symptoms

  ____

- Change in appetite (eating more or less)

  ____

- Sadness

  ____

- Others

  ____

Look at your most recent CORE DISTRESS SCALING.

If your scores are at the high end of the scale – CONGRATUALTIONS, your journey has been successful.

You have emerged as a renewed and changed person. You have chosen inner peace, acceptance and happiness regardless of your decision.

Continue reading until you finish the conclusion. You may wish to express some thoughts and feelings using the extra journal pages or your personal journal at this time.

What is your decision? Can you return to this relationship?

It is up to you to answer these questions. *As noted, continue reading until you finish the conclusion.* If you have not made your decision, you may wish to use structured journal writing at this time. Extra journal sheets are provided for you. Or, perhaps you would prefer to discuss the decision-making process with your friend or therapist.

If your scores are not at the high end of the scale – focus on the information given in the afterward and read the conclusion letter. You can then choose the direction of your extended healing journey.

Epilogue

"If you wish the world to become loving and compassionate, become loving yourself. If you wish to diminish fear in the world, diminish your own."
Gary Zukov

If your situation looks like nothing will change, make your decision with a loving heart and a clear head. You may decide that if the person contacts you directly, you will discuss the situation and state what you want in a relationship. This might never happen. You may have enjoyed a visit and realized that you can reconnect without the baggage you previously carried. A more casual connection could be a possibility.

Whether you say yes or no to the relationship, you need also to say, "So be it, I have done my best. I am at peace with myself."

When processing a ***physical*** loss, we work toward the resolution of grief. When resolving a ***living loss*** it seems that we must first comprehend that the process involves some growing and changing as well as acceptance that it is possible to live with, or without, the enforcer. The small, needy child we discovered within the severed relationship, has become a self-motivated adult ready to live life to the fullest, whether or not the bonds of that desired connection is continued.

You comprehend there is a better understanding of the differences between what you want and what you can achieve in life. The pain has lifted from your heart, your perception is clear and you are better able to look with awe at the wonders of life. You feel lightness in the resolving of a ***living loss.***

Afterword

If there still has been no contact from the enforcer, and you feel the need for closure, you may want to write a letter in order to express your deep feelings. You will not send this letter. A sample letter is included at the conclusion to this book. You may wish to write a similar letter and read it to your therapist or a close friend.

It will be interesting to read the letters you have written during this healing journey. At this time, you may wish to burn all letters after reading. It is up to you. As well, you might need to forgive the enforcer so ***you*** can move forward in your life.

Forgiveness - In a different light

If you feel stuck in anger and unable to ***let go*** at this point, you may need to consider the journey of forgiveness. This forgiveness is for ***YOU*** and not the other person. You will not correspond or talk about forgiveness with the enforcer. It is strictly a process that will help ***you*** move forward in your life. Forgiveness will give you the ability to rid yourself of the baggage from this toxic relationship.

The books in the bibliography, especially Forgiveness (How to Make Peace with Your Past and Get on With your Life) by Dr. Sidney B. Simon will help you move on to this next level of transformation you may need to make. The *enforcer* is not involved in this step. If you feel there is no hope for the relationship, focus on forgiving through saying the following:

"I do truly offer forgiveness to (name the person) and I believe that my enforcer does the best he/she can. I believe there is no further hope that this relationship can survive. ***On the other hand, I wish to clearly state that I believe that the action taken was wrong. Resolution of deep pain was very difficult.*** I am forgiving ***for myself.*** I need to move forward with my life. I believe the enforcer is not solely responsible for the estrangement. I have grown emotionally and spiritually. I am better physically. I no longer look at the situation as a crisis. I see opportunities to move ahead and be the best I can be within the loving and healthy relationships that surround me."

If you feel that your grief is still unresolved, perhaps you would benefit from pursuing self development courses. Options to explore are: co-dependency, adult children of alcoholics, assertiveness training, self esteem courses, forgiveness and communication. Learning new relaxation techniques is another great option. The journey of self improvement is a rewarding experience.

You will find a letter to the enforcer on the next page. You may wish to write a similar letter to him/her. This letter is written for yourself as a summary for the work you have done through this book. As noted previously, this letter is not for mailing/sending. The reading, strategies and exercises have brought you to the end of your healing journey.

Conclusion

"We may not ever understand why we suffer or be able to control the forces that cause our suffering, but we can have a lot to say about what the suffering does to us, and what sort of people we become because of it."
Harold S. Kushner

Dear ____________

I would much rather have a conversation with you. I do sincerely understand and respect your choice to have no contact with me, although, I do sometimes find the estrangement sad.

I realize that we are both responsible. At one point, I unfairly blamed you for our estrangement and took no responsibility. I accept that I feel like an outsider from the family circle. My feelings are real. I am not a neurotic person. I have accepted that, without direct verbal communication, nothing will change.

I have opened my heart to communicate with you, however I am not ready to walk into a situation that remains the same. I am a different person through processing my loss of a relationship with you. I have accepted many things.

I am more grateful than ever for my life. I have so much to be thankful for - a wonderful immediate family, and many friends. What I have received, through this journey, is a deep inner peace. I do understand that I have always wanted more love from you than you were able to give.

My life is one of talking out my problems and openly communicating. I cannot expect the same from you. I feel it is unlikely that there will be further discussions with you. Please understand, if that possibility arises, I am available to you.

I can honestly say that I have no malice or anger toward you. I do know that I have always loved you. Differing opinions are not judgments. It has taken a lot of processing but I am happy where I am in my life.

The estrangement has run deeply and I have felt alienated from my small, extended family. This void has been filled with those who do love and appreciate me. Through this journey I have learned so much about life and myself. I can now truly say I wish you all the best. I love you.

Love, ______________________

Additional Journal Pages

Journal Entry

Date:

Journal Entry

Date:

Journal Entry

Date:

Journal Entry

Date:

Journal Entry

Date:

Journal Entry

Date:

Journal Entry

Date:

About The Author

Barbara Rombough feels everyone deserves to be self developed and happy. The journey of self improvement is deeply rewarding, though at times, difficult. With daily meditation, her journey became more mindful at the age of thirty-eight. Ms. Rombough is still forging new path-ways for herself as she helps others. This is her first published book. Barbara has produced visualization and healing CDs. For more information contact her at www.innerguidedhealing.com. Barbara is a family therapist, M.Ed., in private practice. She lives with her husband in New Brunswick, Canada.

Bibliography

Adams, Christine A. One Day at a Time Therapy. Abbey Press. Indiana. 1990

Bach, David. Jonathan Livingstone Seagull. Avon Books. New York, New York. 1970

Beattie, Melody. Codependent No more and Beyond. Hazelton Publishing. New York, New York. 1989

Benson, Herbert, MD and Eileen Stuart, RN. The Wellness Book Simon and Schuster. 1992

Bradshaw, John. Family Secrets. Bantam Books. New York, New York. 1995

Brewer, Sarah, MD. Simply Relax. Duncan Baird Publishing. 2000

Carlson, Richard and Joseph Bailey. Slowing Down to the Speed of Life. Harper Publishing. San Francisco. 1997

Chodren, Pema. The Place That Scares You. A Guide to Fearlessness in Difficult Times. Shamballa Library. 1987

Engelhardt, Lisa. Acceptance Therapy. Abbey Press, Indiana. 1992

Gawain, Shakti. Creative Visualization. Bantam Publishing. New York, New York. 1985

Gilbert, Laynee. I Remember You. A Grief Journal. San Jose, California. L.O.A. Publications. 2000

Glasser, William, MD

Control Theory. A New Explanation of How We Control Our Lives. Harper & Row. New York, New York. 1989

Choice Theory: A New Psychology of Personal Freedom. New York, New York. Harper & Row. 1999

Hanson, Peter, MD. The Joy of Stress. Hanson Stress Management Organization. 1985

Jeffers, Susan. Feel The Fear and Do It Anyway. Fawcett-Columbine. 1987

Kent, Anne. The Modern Book of Massage. Dell Publishing. New York, New York. 1995.

McGilvery, Carole. et al. The Encyclopedia of Aromatherapy, Massage and Yoga". Ann's Publishing Limited. 2001

Ramsey, Ronald, MD and Rene Noorbergen. Living with Loss. A Dramatic New Breakthrough in Grief Therapy. William Morrow and Company, Inc. New York, New York. 1981

Roger, John and Peter McWilliams. Do It. Prelude Press. 1991.

Seaward, Brian Luke, Ph.D. Stand Like Mountain, Flow Like Water Health Communications. 1997

Servan-Schreiber, David, MD. Anticancer: A New Way of Life. Penguin Group. New York, New York. 2009.

Simon, Sidney, MD and Suzanne Simon. Forgiveness: How to Make Peace with your Past and Get On With Your Life. Warner Books Inc. New York, New York. 1990

Subby, Robert. Lost in the Shuffle. The Co-dependent Reality. Health Comm., Inc. 1987

Urban, Hal. Life's Greatest Lessons. Simon and Schuster. 2003.

Wubbolding, Robert. Reality Therapy for the 21st Century. Harper & Row. 2000.

Internet Resources

www.tearsandhealing.com

www.allaboutcounseling.com

- Co-dependency
- Overview

www.codependents.org

CODA Groups

- Information available through alcoholism services

www.phrases.org.uk/bulletinboard

- Blood is thicker than water

www.webmd.com

www.helpguide.org

- Stress relaxation techniques

www.helpinghandinstitute.com

- Grief Workshops, seminars, lectures
- Daniel Baker, B.Ed., Certified Grief Recovery Specialist

www.innerguidedhealing.com

- Resource Site – Relaxation CDs, books, self help information
- Barbara Rombough, M.Ed., Family Therapist

www.monctonrealitytherapy.ca

- Links for the William Glasser Institute
- Maureen Craig McIntosh, M.Ed., Owner/Director Moncton Reality Therapy Consultants